Crushed

Dominic Moore

BookLeaf Publishing

Presentation by *BookLeaf Publishing*

Web: www.bookleafpub.com

E-mail: info@bookleafpub.com

ISBN: 9789357740951

First edition 2023

*To the squad, my high school English
teachers, and the poets.*

a lot.

A couple months left and I have even more to
do.
Colleges send "you up?" emails,
phone buzzes at 2am
and I answer.
It's 10 in 9 more minutes,
I have to leave for work but I haven't 8 yet,
Getting off at 7,
Hopefully I have enough time around 5
So I can practice my 4N6 pieces,
the routine is in pieces, 3 tourneys to prepare 4,
I mean 4 tourneys,
work again at 5 I'm counting backwards,
stumbling forward.
School's out around 3, my afternoons free.
I'm hoping 2 relax, but I should practice
Or apply for another scholarship,
I'm not the only 1 who's stressed,
But it feels like I'm thought of as 0,
When my expectations are set to 10.

vinyl.

Somedays I feel like an album.
A story sang,
one beautiful listen.
Others, I feel like a scratched vinyl.
I can't sing because words
stick to my throat,
the story goes unsung.

dizzy.

I have this tendency to get dizzy
when life spins too fast.
Everything seems to be my last,
my minds shook,
feet off the ground.
Just another day in
tornado alley.

self care.

Self care is
rest
after an hour of
math test cramming.
Self care is
a steaming bowl of soup
on a cold winter day.
Self care is hot cocoa
after tears turn to headaches, warming
your throat when every word cuts like barbed
wire.
Self care is daydreaming,
when you only have nightmares.
Self care is learning to love yourself
when your mind is failing that lesson.
Self care is an essential,
the most important step in a healthy head.

these hands.

These wrists bruise easy
while they
rest on the edge of my keyboard,
going numb as each minute passes.

My thumbs press the bar,
jamming,
desperately trying
to find space to fit
an I love you in between
words that don't begin to describe how I feel.

My fingers move furiously,
twitching and shaking
with each letter and enter pressed,
I feel more stressed
because for you I try to do everything perfect.

These nails get chipped away by teeth,
and call it disgusting
but it's a habit that one who
anxiously awaits loves call
picks up while on hold.

This poem was supposed to be one line,

how I felt about you.
I knew I loved you but
that didn't feel like enough,
so I remembered that love is a sweet pain
that I'd politely ask to leave
but when it refuses I know
I'd never show it the door.

puzzle.

Your house is empty now.
The walls are painted with memories,
and the air echoes of your lost laugh,
stories you once told. Your smile
shines brighter
through pictures
to compensate for your absence.
We sit in your living room,
visiting,
but something's missing.
Someone's missing.
An unfinished puzzle sits on the table.
When you died,
we didn't bother to put the rest together.
We knew even if we tried-
still a piece missing.

nobody will read this.

Now I write, another love poem
Or the havoc in my head. Writing about
Beautiful scenes,
Or the seasons.
Does it matter?
Years pass,
While
I
Look at all the people I
Love
Remain here. They say college is
Exciting
And I'm not sure I buy it, I'm scared to
Death. I'm
Trying to
Hold onto the time
I have left,
Smiling now, knowing it's not long til curtain
call.

an ode to an autumn goodbye.

This is an ode to apple pie,
whose warm crust and crisp cinnamon apples
make my mouth water.

To hot chocolate,
keeping me warm,
when the world seems so cold.

To homemade chicken noodle soup
with grocery store rotisserie chicken.

To families by blood and by choice,
those who accept
and love all.

To the empty streets on Halloween night,
that aren't littered with children and candy
wrappers, it's not you,
it's the powered off porch lights.

To Thanksgiving eve,
the calm before the storm of
aggressive politics, clenched fists
and tears over pumpkin pies.

To Thanksgiving,
I apologize that you are the middle child of
holidays,
and that people like your brother Christmas
better.

To the bleachers of the student section,
when the stray fists hit you during the fight,
I'm sorry nobody
asked if you were ok.

Again to the trees,
adoring your falling colors is the best way
to celebrate a wonderful life not yet finished.

To pumpkin spice coffee,
I may be basic for my love of you,
but I need a seasonal sugar rush.

To movie nights with friends,
that I wish would never end.

To the season that is in between summer and
winter,
Do you prefer to be called
Autumn or Fall?

To all the things I love and lose this time of year,

I wrote this poem as a love letter to you,
knowing it would never reach your hands.

on the way to a funeral.

Empty trees,
desolate roads,
roadkill and burnt rubber,
on the sides of highways
that haven't seen love in years.
The sun,
a patch of blinding yellow,
incapable today of taking a true shape.
Billboards advertising freedom for sale
and winding streets with falling leaves,
twirling ballerinas.
Balloons of love floating away, mindlessly
drifting.

At a funeral,
pulling into the parking lot of tears,
opening the door
to look at memories.
Why is it that family moves closer into frame
when a member leaves the picture?
Taking seats in velvet pews,
blank and blotchy faces all around.
Struggling to keep it together myself,
as people gift tears at the casket.

At a burial,
nearly sprained ankles, tripping,
dress shoes on dry dirt.
Vibrant pinks and purples,
flowers everywhere,
like the gardens she used to tend to.

On the way home from a funeral,
singing showtunes
after stopping for tacos at
the place we once loved.
Going to a rest stop bathroom,
looking at scribbled politics and graffiti on the
wall.
Arriving home,
untucking my shirt,
and checking the mail.
I look up at the moon, hiding behind thin clouds,
to say goodbye one last time.

life is a fairytale.

when you keep company
with poison apples.
Cold hearts frozen over,
Snow White.

Life is a fairytale
when love is blind.
Trying to read signs
with eyes
pecked out by grim ravens.

Life is a fairytale
when nobody lets their hair down
no matter how many times
you beg for Rapunzel.

Life is a fairytale
when you close the book.
When you've told your story
to an empty crowd.

hurricane.

"Kids! We need to talk."
A day like any other.
Rains gentle kiss
hit the glass windows.
The type of day that begs
to be spent in bed.
I unravel the covers of my bed
and run downstairs.
I look out in the dining room,
the comfort I once had disappeared.
My parents are at the table,
but something about it feels empty.
My mom sits,
eyes holding back water like doomed levees.
My father says,
Have a seat.
I finally caught on,
"I don't want you to get a divorce!"
The levees in my mother's eyes finally broke,
and my father's tears fell too.
I finally took a seat,
the salty water from my eyes
flooded my face.
I felt betrayed
and I knew it was selfish.

I didn't see it then
but they were actually helping.
I realized that day,
that sometimes it takes a hurricane
to build something back great.

snow on the trees.

I pray for the branches
of trees in the winter.
Ice glazes twigs,
while snow bends the sticks.
Most snap under the weight,
but praise to the ones that won't break.

cavemen.

Poets must tighten their language,
"too many word no good,
word no good."
Critiques are a belt constantly fastening,
choking creativity and strangling syllables,
"fewer word better,
little is best."
As if pouring out your heart
in ink
or lead
or text on a screen
should be limited by
the fewest words you can possibly write.
"Silence is best,
write don't speak."
But to write is to speak
for those who can't
or won't
or don't know how.
"Quiet writer,
cry louder."
Tear, dropped paper into trashcans
masks the sound of teardrops
hitting my notepad.
"Tighten language,

choke on words."
I'm suffocating on my line breaks,
I hope this poem was worth it.
Now you have a writer
who doesn't know
what the worth of his word is.

no resolution.

I spent
three hours and forty seven minutes
of my New Year's Eve
thinking of the perfect resolution.
Something achievable or within reach,
but still something I can work towards.
I look into last years shattered mirror,
shards of a broken promise,
and decided not to make one.
If I did,
it would be
I'm never lying to myself again.

foggy.

I've always been the person
who needs to have everything
on a schedule,
the unexpected is my enemy.
Sometimes my life feels like
I'm shining a flashlight into the fog,
searching for what's next,
but all I find is that my light is gone.

crushing.

Your name is tied to my tongue
like my shoestrings are knotted together.
I'm tripping over words describing how I fell for
you.
I don't hit the ground,
instead, the clouds.
Once I've landed I look out at the sunset.
Beautiful colors tucked under
wispy white pillows.
Every time I look into your eyes
I have trouble standing.
If this is how it feels falling for you,
look at me.
I want to trip again.

fatigue.

No rest is left for the artists,
each day is different paint
on the same canvas.

nostalgia is one hell of a drug.

A friend taught me how to
smoke my memories,
and I'm becoming an addict.
Stories create contact highs
that seep bittersweetly into my mind.
My name is Dom.
I've lost myself in my past.

on an island.

25

floating
on my own little island.
Ink oceans and
crumpled paper beach balls
rule my lonely paradise.

falling behind.

26

Every time I hold your hand,
my heart races.
We kiss and you rest your head
on my chest,
you hear it beating.
It's trying to
catch up to the fact
that somebody as breathtaking
as you loves me.

an ode to the writers.

27

To the authors
whose words speak volumes
before they finish a page.
To the poets
who put their hearts faults
into each line break.
To all the writers
who don't believe in their stories,
keep writing. It deserves to be told.